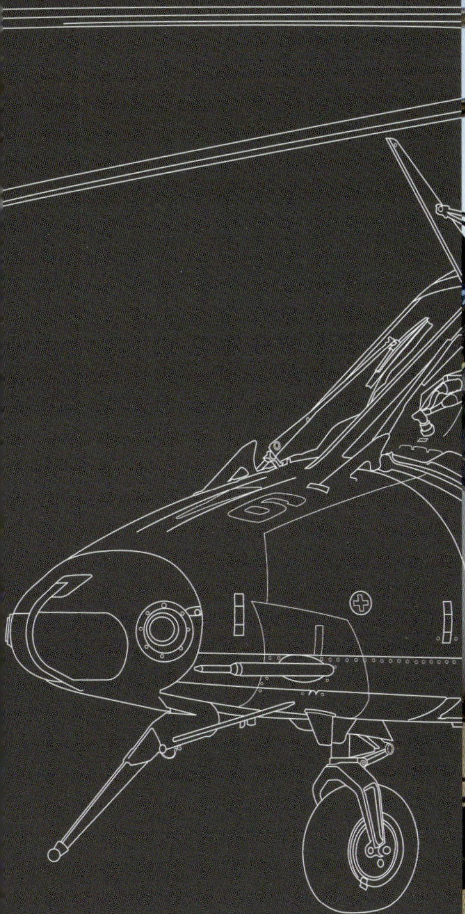

Photo: Gert Trachez

AgustaWestland A109

AgustaWestland A109

This 24th book in our series is a rather special one. Not only is it an in-depth photographic portrait of the Agusta – or nowadays AgustaWestland – A109 light helicopter, but also a presentation of the much-loved A109 Demo Team of the Belgian Air Force. The timing of this book is no coincidence; at the time of writing, the A109 celebrated it's 30th anniversary of service within the Belgian Air Force. As a tribute to the team, the first 45 pages of this book are on the Demo Team, which in 2022 is lead by Sr. Cpt. Jo Jacobs. This book wouldn't have been possible without the help of Jo and his entire team.

The A(W)109 has proven itself to being a popular helicopter, both in military and civilian service. In the past few decades, the type has seen some extensive modifications, most of which we will show you in the second part of this book which also contains the walk-around of the helicopter. The early version, which is in use with the Belgian Air Force has a fixed landing gear and the initial type of engine exhausts, while the newer versions, such as those in use with the Swedish Air Force or New Zealand Air Force have a retractable landing gear and a different exhaust lay-out. The A109 has been and remains a reliable light helicopter, doing its job far away from the spotlights. This however changes with this book, where we put it centre show.

Quite a few people have helped with the photographs for this book. In the first place, I'd like to thank Bart Rosselle, the former official photographer of the Belgian Air Force, who has retired in the last year and is now touring Europe with a much too large RV. A big thank you to Gert Trachez, Kris Christiaens and Andy Heap as well, the latter for providing us with some stunning photographs of the New Zealand A109s. I hope that you enjoy this book on an often-overlooked type. You'll notice that it is a helicopter well worth 116 pages!

Photo: Jörgen Nillson

Special thanks to: Bart Rosselle, Robert Pied, Kris Christiaens, Gert Trachez, Peter Anthoni, Jeroen van Veenendaal, Marc Talloen, Laurent Heyligen, Jörgen Nillson, Gunter Geens, Andy Heap, the Belgian Air Force, the entire A109 Demo Team and the many enthusiastic photographers that sent the team photos.

Photo: Kris Christiaens

Photo: Bart Rosselle

An Agusta A-109 demonstration team is one of the traditions of the modern Belgian Air Force. The photo above shows the team's livery in 2021. The photo to the right shows the paint scheme that the team's helicopter was flown in in 2012 sporting the Spartan King Leonidas on the port side - the symbol of 18 Squadron. On the starboard side, it carried the Griffin of 17 Squadron.

Photo: Laurent Heyligen

Helicopters can be tasked in many different ways, from transport to liaison or observation. This is also the case with the A109, even though it is a light helicopter. Early on, Agusta developed several versions of the type; like the liaison helicopter that was bought by the Belgian Air Force – photo above – or the rescue helicopter used in the Swiss Alps – photo to the right. Look at the different type of exhaust and the different landing gear of the latter, enabling it to land in the snow.

Photo: Philip Stevens

Photo: Gert Trachez

A Belgian Air Force A109 is spectacularly dropping flares. Initially taken on by the Belgian Army, the light helicopter was used in a variety of tasks, from observation and liaison to anti-tank missions in close air support to ground troops. Medevac missions were also included in the tasks, and for this, A109s with a widened fuselage were ordered. When the helicopters were transferred to the Belgian Air Force in 2004 and re-stationed first at Bierset Air Base and later at Beauvechain Air Base, the type of tasks changed, as well as some of the equipment. Anti-tank missiles were no longer used, but the light helicopter could still be equipped with machine guns, positioned in the cargo bay, aft of the cockpit.

A109 variants & operators

Ever since the A109 has been introduced in 1971, many variants of the helicopter have been built. The initial A109A was called 'Hirundo', which is Latin for 'Swallow, and came into service with the Italian Army. The Belgian version was designated A109BA. The photo to the right shows the Swedish variant, the A109LUH – Light Utility Helicopter – which is based on the A109E, an upgraded version powered by two Pratt & Whitney PW206C engines.

Photo: Jörgen Nillson

Photo: Gert Trachez

Belgian Air Force Agusta Display Team

The Belgian Air Force has a long tradition to represent its capabilities during air shows; remember the very successful F-16 Dark Falcon Display Team, on which we have published a limited edition book, back in 2019. Another much-appreciated team is the A109 Display Team, which has been around for many years. In 2021 the otherwise green livery of the A109 picked by the team, was exchanged for a spectacular grey and black splinter scheme, designed by Jeroen van Veenendaal. Sporting on either side of the fuselage is a huge wolf, the insignia of the 1 Wing, where the unit is based. The team adopted the name ‘Razzle Blades” and the helicopter is flown by Sr. Cpt. Jo Jacobs and Sr. Cpt. Stijn Soenens, who together have almost 4.000 flying hours on the type. For the 2022 season, the team added a stylised logo on the vertical tail, celebrating the 30th anniversary of the type in service within the Belgian Air Force. A team of 5 ground crew supports the two pilots, making sure the helicopter is always in perfect condition.

Photo: Gert Trachez

Photo: Gert Trachez

Above: The official team photo of the 2022 Razzle Blades A109 Display Team, with the two pilots in the middle looking very happy that they can once again perform their spectacular display, after the forced inactivity during the Covid-19 years. Their loyal team members are from left to right: Yves, Yaron, Scott, J.J., Stijn, Thomas and Koen.

Left: The team even has a spectacular team car in the form of this Mustang that often travels with the team to air shows. Hard to remain unnoticed in that one!

Photo: Patrick Bertaux

Versatile for over 30 years

The first A109s for the Belgian Army were delivered in 1992, 4 years after a contract was signed to acquire 46 of the type to replace the ageing Alouette II helicopter. Initially, the helicopters were used in the Armed Reconnaissance role and for observation tasks, but could also be equipped with Helitow anti-tank missiles, or be employed as a light transport or Medevac helicopter. When in 2004 the helicopters were handed over to the Belgian Air Force, they were brought up to the same multi-role standard and operated by 17 and 18 Squadron.

Some of the 46 initial machines have been put into storage, some have been sold. Today, just 10 remain in active service. After a service of 3 decades, the Belgian Air Force is considering a replacement for the little agile helicopter. One of the contenders for this is Eurocopter's H145.

Right: Jo Jacobs – left – and Stijn Soenens – right – pose with their custom painted helmets in front of their helicopter in the spring of 2022. Both are experienced pilots, with respectively 1,800 and over 2,000 flying hours on the type. Outside of the airshow season, they are instructor pilots attached to 17 Squadron, based at Beauvechain Air Base. Their helicopter, with registration H46, was the last to be delivered to the Belgian Air Force, in February of 1994.

Photo: Gert Trachez

Photo: Marc Talloen

Left: Early 2021 and the A109 of the Demo Team is about to land at its home base of Beauvechain. The impressive show of the team shows just how agile and manoeuvrable the light helicopter actually is and what an important asset it is for the Belgian Air Force, even after 30 years of service. The base is also the home of 4 NH90 TTH medium size helicopters and a fleet of SF.260 Marchetti training aircraft, which have been in service with the Belgian Air Force for over 50 years. In the last couple of years, the Belgian Air Force has decided to replace almost all of its assets; F-16s will be replaced by F-35As, the C-130 have been exchanged for the much bigger and more capable A400M Atlas. It won't be long before the A109 too will be replaced.

Photo: Jeroen Van Veenendaal

Photo: Jeroen Van Veenendaal

Above: Designing and painting the helicopter was a challenge and for this, the team could rely on the work of the Beauvechain paint shop and the talent of Jeroen Van Veenendaal, who made the spectacular splinter design for the team. In this photo, you see the A109 on it's cradle, with both rotors removed and the wolf's heads about to be painted on.

Left: The first thing that was to do for the Beauvechain paintshop team, is the unglorious task of sanding down some of the paint of the airframe and masking off all of the glass areas and some of the vital parts. The Belgian Air Force A109s have a fixed landing gear, so this too has to be protected. Doors and cargo doors have been removed.

AgustaWestland A109
BAF Display Team

Photo: Demo Team BAF

It's one thing to make a design for an aircraft or a helicopter - and not to be taken for granted - but it is another to get it on the machines. This can't be done without the expertise of the people of the paintshop; sanding down the airframe, working from a plan, hours and hours of masking, painting, some more masking, plotting the designs, etc. So, here's a big thank you to them !

Photo: Demo Team BAF

Photo: Gert Trachez

Left: For the 2022 season, the team added a special marking to the vertical tail of their '46' which celebrates the 30th anniversary of the type in service with the Belgian Air Force. It makes the helicopter look even smarter than it was already!

Photo: Marc Talloen

From the cockpit

Seen from the crowd line, the demonstration flight of the Razzle Blades is spectacular - imagine what it looks like from the cockpit. Well, the photo above give you a good idea. While Jo is banking hard right towards the crowd, Stijn keeps an eye on the instruments and the order of the manoeuvres. Look at the different position of the dual instruments on the instrument panel. The display itself holds some very impressive manoeuvres, with the helicopter being flown in a 90 degrees downwards angle while flares are being dropped or nose up until it stalls followed by a right hand side slide and recovery. The display underlines just how agile the 30+ years old helicopter performs. Notice the Airspeed Limitations chart on the top right canopy frame. The photo is actually a still from a film made by Marc Talloen, a well known and talented camera operator with a much visited youtube chanel, who often combines parts of the show seen from te ground with cockpit shots.

Photo: Kris Christiaens

Photo: Gert Trachez

Above: Coming back after their 10-minute display and about to land at their home base of Beauvechain. Look at the reflection of the red anti-collision light, placed on top of the fuselage.

Right: Banking in the early sun in March 2022, the Razzle Blades helicopter sits on the tarmac, sporting the '30 Years' logo on the vertical tail.

Photo: Gert Trachez

Above: Basking in the spring sunlight of 2022, the Razzle Blades H46 is ready for another season. Notice the “30 Years” logo on the vertical tail.

Photo: Gert Trachez

Right: The pilots of the team are eager to show the helicopter’s capabilities during the 2022 season. As ambassadors for the Belgian Air Force, they answer perfectly to the profile for the job: accessible to the public, humble and ready to take the time to answer any questions of the public. They are the inspiration for many youngsters to become a pilot themselves.

Photo: Kris Christiaens

Above: For the benefit of aircraft spotters, the Team's helicopter has been powered up for a photo shoot at dusk. The anti-collision lights on top and underneath the fuselage and the navigation lights near the tail rotor are lit. Such events are important for the Belgian Air Force, generating much enthusiasm. The goal is to push recruitment; like so many air forces, the Belgian Air Force has difficulty finding motivated people.

Photo: Gert Trachez

Right: H46 is pushed backwards out of the maintenance hangar, ready for a test flight. The crew doors are already open and the technical team is on stand-by to load the flares into the dispensers, located below the cargo doors.

Photo: Tom Houquet

Photo: Marc Talloen

Above: H46 poses behind a photoship during the 2021 Sanicole Airshow in Belgium. With the landing lights on, it looks even more spectacular! The menacing wolf on either side of the fuselage seems to be ready to devour anyone who comes in sight.

Right: This is what it's all about: flying their awesome display and seen from the cockpit, it is even more breathtaking than from the crowd line. In this photo, J.J. – Sr. Cpt. Jo Jacobs – is pointing the nose down almost 90 degrees, while Stijn is standing by to release flares.

Right: Keeping control of the A109, even when pushing the helicopter to its limits shows the skills of the two pilots. Here, going through zero G, J.J. pushed the nose downwards while flares are being dropped. As you can imagine, doing the show at a sunset airshow, makes a really spectacular display.

Photo: Yaron Allaert

Below: Yaron Allaert made this very cool photo in 2021, flying alongside H46 against a thunderous sky. Apparent in this photo are the fully extended landing gear, the black-and-white tail rotor and the impressive wolfs head that seems to be on fire. The work of designer Jeroen van Veenendaal executed by the team of the Beauvechain paint shop.

Photo: Yaron Allaert

Photo: Gert Trachez

Teamwork !

A display team is so much more than the pilots performing their show. Being very much aware of the important work they do, the pilots rely on the professionalism and talent of the 5 technicians assigned to the team. Each of them volunteers for the job and takes care of the technical side of H46 on top of their daily work. They make sure that the A109 is in top shape whenever the team is performing, whether it is in Belgium or abroad. Rightfully so, they proudly carry the slogan on the back of their sweaters “No techs no flights”.

Photo: Gert Trachez

Photo: Gert Trachez

Photo: Gert Trachez

Above: A technician has gone up the steps on the side of the fuselage to check the main rotor's mechanism. Everything on the A109 can be checked without the help of special ladders or equipment, allowing the basic checks to be carried out even when the helicopter lands outside an airfield. While on the ground, a static line is attached to the fuselage. Notice the completely filled flare dispenser.

Left: One of the team's technicians is putting a Remove Before Flight tag on the fuselage, aft of the refuelling point. The wooden crates next to him hold the flares that will be used during the display and are to be fixed in the dispensers, located underneath the cargo door on either side of the fuselage. When the helicopter is parked, covers are placed on intakes and exhausts, preventing FOD – Foreign Object Damage. Notice the closed steps on the fuselage and compare the position with the photo above.

Duke Hawkins 024

Photo: Gert Trachez

AgustaWestland A109 BAF Display Team

Left: How about this for a glamour shot? Freshly out of the Beauvechain paintshop with the brand new "30 Years" logo on the vertical tail, H46 is ready for the 2022 season. The helicopter's number is painted in dark grey on the nose, while the Belgian insignia is painted on the crew entrance doors. This photo shows to good effect that only the pilot, sitting in the right seat, has a window over him. Look how narrow the yellow-tipped rotor blades actually are.

Below: H46 is pushed back into the main hangar at Beauvechain Air Base by one of the team's technicians. In the background, a standard dark green A109 can be seen in maintenance. See how a metal protection is placed around the nose landing gear? We'll tell you more about the reason why in the maintenance chapter in this book! Look how the rotor tips of the Razzle Blades helicopter are protected by a yellow cover and a Remove Before Flight tag.

Photo: Gert Trachez

Photo: Gert Trachez

Photo: Gert Trachez

Above: 2021 and at one of the few airshows that were attended - we were still at the height of a global pandemic - the pilots of the A109 Demo Team release a pair of flares. Flares are an important part of the show of the team, especially when performing near sundown. Underneath the two cargo doors, flare dispensers have been installed by the ground crew. Flares are actually a self-defence system used by helicopters and aircraft. When fired upon by heat-seaking missiles that are going after the engine's heat, the flares act as a decoy. The missiles go for the heat generated by the flares, giving the helicopter a chance to escape.

Right: A close-up of one of the flare dispensers installed on the team's A109. This dispenser holds 30 flares and with one of these on either side of the A109, a maximum of 60 flares can be dropped.

Photo: Gert Trachez

Above: Proudly presenting the 2022 Razzle Blades A109 Demo Team of the Belgian Air Force, from left to right: Koen, Thomas, Scott, Yaron, J.J., Stijn and Yves.

Photo: Gert Trachez

Left: Standing at a safe distance while Stijn and J.J. go through the necessary checks before they start the engines of their faithful H46. Whenever the team is performing outside the country, equipment and spare parts have to be transported to the venue by the team's technicians who are all volunteers.

Photo: Gert Trachez

Above: This may well be the Belgian Air Force's A109 Demo Team's helicopter, that doesn't mean it isn't used during normal operations. And like any of the A109s in the fleet, maintenance has to be done on it. Notice the forward engine cover to the right in the photo.

Photo: Gert Trachez

Right: Before every flight - no matter if it is an operational flight or a demonstration flight - the ground crew team checks the vital parts of the helicopter. Here, two of them are checking the engine and some access panels, making sure everything is the way it is supposed to be. And it is like it is written on the back of their vests: "No techs, no flights". Look at the colour of the exhausts in this photo.

Photo: Kris Christiaens

Left: Time for a test-flight. It's a rainy day, but that doesn't matter a lot for the enthusiastic crew, that has been preparing the helicopter for this moment. Next will be the acceptance flight in front of the brass and if they say it's a go, the airshow season can really start. Taken at slow speed, this photograph shows the A109 taxiing towards it's take off spot. Look at the reflection of the anti-collision light on the main rotor and the blades.

Right: In order to get to the rotor and the engines, steps are located on either side of the helicopter that fold down, above and below the refuelling point. Look at how detailed the paintjob is of the wolf's head in this photo.

Far right: One of the team's ground crew is making sure the Remove Before Flight tags are all removed before the flight crew arrives for a test flight. Strict procedures are to be followed when flying military aircraft and helicopters; routine is nowhere near these machines.

Photo: Gert Trachez

Photo: Gert Trachez

Photo: Gert Trachez

Left: Before 2021, the A109 team flew in an almost standard dark green livery – in this case in airframe H29. I say almost, because the fuselage sported a low-viz wolf design on either side… In this impressive photo by Gert Trachez, the helicopter is dropping flares. Smoke coming from the latter is curling up by the turbulence created by the rotor blades, making the shot even more spectacular. During the display, the landing lights are usually kept on.

Below: During a training session at a snowy homebase of Beauvechain, the team is preparing for another airshow season. The attentive observer might notice the equipment placed on the helicopter's nose; this is a VXP sensor, which is used during maintenance flights to measure the main rotor blade balance. Afterwards, the balance of the blades can be adjusted if necessary. We'll show you the details of the sensor further on page 50.

Airshow !

Photo: Jozef Vanden Broeck, BAF

Photo: Gert Trachez

Above: It is a rainy day at Beauvechain Air Base when the team take their helicopter up for a training flight, pre-season. In the distance, the lights on top of the base's main hangars are lit.

Photo: BAF media team

Right: Stijn – left – and J.J. – right – have climbed up the steps on either side of the fuselage to remove the covers and check the engine compartment and main rotor before a training flight. This photo, taken in 2021, shows that the Covid-19 pandemic is still in full swing. Unfortunately, it will be another year before a 'normal' display season will be possible.

Below: Each year, before the start of the airshow season, the display teams of the Belgian Air Force have to present their ambition and show to the Air Force brass during the 'acceptance trials'. For the 2021 season, the 'ambassadors' of the Belgian Air Force were the 'Red Devils', flying 4 Marchetti's SF.260, the 'Razzle Blades' flying the A109 and the Dark Falcon F-16 Display Team, with Stefan "Vador" Darte at the controls of the fighter jet. In this photo, J.J. is explaining the manoeuvres the crowds can expect of the A109 Demo Team. Notice the team's badge on his shoulders and the 17 Squadron insignia on his right chest.

Photo: BAF media team

Photo: Walter Van Bel

Above: The two pilots put their A109 through its paces during a tight right hand turn, while shooting flares. The A109 might be a small helicopter, but spectators are always impressed by the dynamic show the team puts forward. Notice the curved tail rotor protection underneath the vertical tail.

Photo: Kris Christiaens

Another impressive shot of the team's A109 dropping flares during the Sanicole sunset airshow in 2021. The Belgian A109s are – like the civil A109C version of the helicopter – powered by a pair of Allison Model 250-C20R-1 turboshaft engines. This is a widely used and highly reliable engine that powers many small aircraft and helicopters, like the SIAI-Marchetti SF.260 TP, the Aeromacchi M-290, Bell OH-58 Kiowa and the AS350 Ecureuil helicopter to name but a few.

Right: Agusta A109 '46' is being used during regular operations whenever it isn't needed for promotional duties, like airshows, or visiting schools during recrutement campaigns. Here, the helicopter is flying in formation with one of it's stablemates, which is also sporting quite an impressive wolf's head.

Below: The team is directing their helicopter towards the runway for a maintenance flight.

Photo: Jeroen Van Veenendaal

Photo: Jeroen Van Veenendaal

Photo: Jeroen Van Veenendaal

Photo: Tom Houquet

Left: Seemingly popping up from in between the trees, '46' is hovering for the camera. Seen from the front, the splinter camouflage looks really good! Notice the upwards position of the main rotor blades during this manoeuvre and the wide track landing gear, ensuring maximum stability when landing on soft surfaces. Look at the green and red navigation light on the tips of the horizontal tails.

Above: On route over the northern part of Belgium, close to the Army's shooting range of Leopoldsburg. On top and underneath the fuselage, wire cutters are placed in case the helicopter flies through electricity lines during missions. The four main rotor blades turn at a maximum speed of 385 RPM and are 11 m. in diameter with a disc surface of 95 m2. The tail rotor has two blades, with a diameter of 2 m.

Photo: Patrick Vercautteren

High Performance !

Performing at many airshows, Open Doors or Spotter events in Europe, the Agusta Demo Team of the Belgian Air Force is photographed by many aviation enthusiasts. About 2 months before the publication of this book, Sr Cpt. Jo Jacobs posted a request for photos on the team's facebook page. The return was overwhelming: almost immediately photos started coming in and just 20 days after the initial post, almost 5 Gigabytes of photos were sent to the team. Many of these photos were absolutely stunning and some of the photos that stood out for us, were selected. On the next 10 pages, we show you those. A big thank you from the team to everyone who sent in photos!

Photo: Tom Meirlaen

Design: Jeroen van Veenendaal

Design: Jeroen van Veenendaal

The design of the spectacular paintscheme of the A109 Demo Team was developped by Jeroen van Veenendaal, who also made the team's badge, seen to the left. It took some convincing before the people at the Belgian Air Force HQ agreed to abandon the standard green camouflage for this grey-and-black splinter camouflage with a huge stylised wolves head on either side of the fuselage.

Opposite page: An impressive air-to-air shot made by Patrick Vercauteren shows the sleek lines of the A109 - notice the full flare dispenser. Tom Meirlaen pictured the Demo Team's helicopter hovering moments before touching down. Notice the landing lights and the nose up position of the A109.

Photo: Luc Dujardin

How about this for a fantastic shot? Looks as if fire is raining down from the Razzle Blades helicopter. I like the contrast of the dynamic flares with the stillness of the rotor blades due to the high exposure time of the camera. Flares make the show even more spectacular than it already is and many photographers eagerly await the moment they are dropped by the team.

The design of '46' and especially the orange colour around the wolf's head emphasizes the light coming from the flares. This isn't the first design by Jeroen van Veenendaal though; he also created the livery of a Chinook helicopter for the Royal Netherlands Air Force to celebrate the 75th anniversary of 298 Squadron. That heavy transport helicopter sports a bear on one side of the fuselage and a dragonfly on the other.

The display of the team takes just under 10 minutes and includes some breathtaking manoeuvres - you can find some spectacular footage of the display on Youtube - which shows the speed and agility of the helicopter and the professionalism and skills of the two-man crew that has to be perfectly in-sinc during the low-level display. Maybe I should ask for a ride-along with them, but preferably before lunch...

Right: Thomas Devos captured the Razzle Blades helicopter taxiing towards the runway in the early spring of 2021. The show starts with the helicopter coming directly towards the crows at high speed and pulling up into a steep climb during which flares are being dropped. The manoeuvre sets the tone for a spectacular 10 minutes. During the display, the team includes a hovering sequence during which the helicopter spins around its axis, after which it manoeuvres vertically before making a hard right hand 180 degree turn away from the crowd.

Photo: Thomas Devos

Photo: Marc Talloen

Left: J.J. on the left and Stijn on the right are accessable and humble pilots and gladly take the time to talk to aviation enthusiasts and youngsters considering a career as a military pilot during airshows. Of course, the impressive livery of their helicopter adds to the "coolness" of the duo.

Photo: Tom Houquet

Above: This is what a flare drop looks like in the air; ever so spectacular. The display of the Razzle Blades is done in a very small airspace which not only makes it highly dynamic, but also shows the capacity of the helicopter to turn on a dime. For the crew, it's all hunky dory.

Right: An extreme close-up of the port side of the fuselage, showing just how menacing the wolf actually is. Look at the details of the paintjob and the angry look of the eye... It is in stark contrast to the kindness of the two pilots and their 5 technicians, who are always up for a chat.

Photo: Quentin Joschko

AgustaWestland A109
BAF Display Team

Photo:Remco Albring

Above: Bang! A close-up of '46' at exactly the right moment: when it is firing off a huge amount of flares. A great shot by Remco Albring!

Photo: Luc Dujardin

Left: It might not be as loud as an F-16 or a Rafale solo display, but that doesn't mean it is less impressive. The display of the Razzle Blades is quite technical and requires absolute concentration of the two-man crew. In this nicely balanced photo, '46' is sitting on the tarmac of Florennes Air Base in Belgium, waiting for the time to start the show. Note the filled flare dispensers.

Photo: Thomas Devos

Photo: Jozef Vanden Broeck

Above: Taken during a sunset air show, this photo by Thomas Devos shows the A109 team's performce head-on. Notice the landing lights in the nose and the navigation lights on the extremities of the horizontal tails: green on the starboard side, red on the port side.

Right: Team-member Yves is standing by while pilots Jo and Stijn are doing their final cockpit checks. The Razzle Blades are ready for another spectacular performance!

Right: Sanicole Airshow in 2021 and Gijs Mouchaers made this dramatic photo of the A109 droping flares while breaking to the right. The display shows that the helicopter is not only versatile but also extremely manoeuvrable. The light of the flares, reflecting in the main rotor blades makes this such a great shot!

Below: Even when the team's helicoptor is on the ground, some impressive photos can be made of it. Quentin Joschko made this great frontal close-up shot of '46', showing the structure of the nose, the windscreen and the windscreen whipers. Notice the air intake in front of the windscreen and the hinges giving access to the avionics bays in the nose of the A109. The Belgian A109s only have a transparent ceiling part on the starboard side of the cockpit. In the early days, equipment was mounted on top of the port side of the fuselage.

Photo: Quentin Joschko

Photo: Gijs Mouchaers

Photo: Nathalie Ponsonnaille

Photo: Serge Nemry

Above: Taken on a grey day, this great action photo shows the effects of the engine exhausts and the rotor blades, while the helicopter is making a hard left hand turn. Notice that the landing lights in the nose have been illuminated.

Right: Look at these two being all smiles and proud with their Certificate of Official Ambassador of the Belgian Air Force. These are awarded to the display pilots at the beginning of each season.

Photo: Wout Torfs

Photo: Arne Lemaire

Above: Coming out of the cloud created by the flares, the crew is already manoeuvring for the next part in the show. It really doesn't feel like ten minutes of display, because of the high frequency of manoeuvres on a very tight spot. Seeing this, you can see why some refer to this part of the display as the 'Angel Wings'.

Right: A high speed turn at low level also generates opportunities for great shots!

Photo: Gert Trachez

Walkaround

After the presentation of the Belgian Air Force Razzle Blades, it's time to start the walkaround of the AgustaWestland – today Leonardo - A(W)109, something that hasn't been done before. And that's a shame, because the light helicopter is an interesting one in many aspects. First of all, it is highly versatile and this is why so many different versions of it have been developped since the first one was introduced over 50 years ago and why it is still in production today. Initially, Agusta planned it as a single-engine helicopter, but quite early in the design phase, it seemed more prudent to equip it with two engines. For this, the Allison 250-C14 turboshaft engine was selected. When it was introduced, the popular Bell 206 was nearing the end of its career, so for the Italian company, their new A109 came at the perfect moment. While the helicopter kept being upgraded, Agusta and Westland helicopters merged in July of 2000, resulting in the new designation AW109.

The A109 proved to be popular both in civilian use and government use, with helicopters being delivered to private operators and VIP transport companies as well as customs services, rescue services, police, the military and many more. Today, the type can be equipped with a variety of power plants as well as other equipment, such as winching systems, GPS systems, flotation devices, a weather radar ... The A109 can be flown under single or dual pilot configuration and if requested, the military version can be equipped with weapon systems, such as gun pods, cannons or even air-to-air missiles, even though this is highly unusual. So let's have a closer look at the A109, shall we?

In 2011, the New Zealand Air Force acquired 6 AW109s, of which two are seen in the photo above. Of interest is that these helicopters have been equipped with a winching system, located on the starboard side of the fuselage. Because the helicopter is rather small in size, it looks a little odd, no? The New Zealand Air Force uses the type to train future helicopter pilots, en route to flying the NH90 medium sized transport helicopter.

Photo: Gert Trachez

Photo: Duke Archiv

Above and below: Initially, the Belgian A109s were equipped with a targeting pod located on the port side, on top of the fuselage and used when engaging tanks and military vehicles with missiles. When this capacity was no longer necessary, these pods were removed. This is the reason why the Belgian A109s only have one window in their roofs.

Tradition dictates that we start with the forward fuselage of our subjects, so let's do just that. The photo above shows the sleek nose of the A109 BA as it is in service with the Belgian Air Force. The helicopter sits rather low on its landing gear, which is why the flight crew can get into the cockpit by opening a typical car door. On either side of the nose, Radar Warning Receivers are placed. The nose houses avionics, which can easily be accessed by means of lateral doors which open upwards. Further in this book, we'll show you what can be found inside. Notice the small air intake in the middle of the nose, in front of the windscreen.

Photo: Gert Trachez

Photo: Gert Trachez

Above: A lot of interesting details in this close-up of the forward port fuselage. Notice the elegant nose of the helicopter - it is an Italian design - with the large access doors on top of it. Immediately below, a pitot tube is located. Forward of the door, the black round Radar Warning Receiver can be seen. Underneath the nose, a wire cutter is installed. Another one can be found above the windscreen. The co-pilot's door hinges forward, while the cargo bay door slides backwards. Both on top and below the fuselage, communication antennas are located.

Left: This photo shows the dedication of Gert Trachez when taking photos: lying on the ground, looking up, this is the nose of the A109 with the dual landing light and protective bar in front of it. Notice the position of the Radar Warning Receivers.

Photo: Gert Trachez

Photo: Gert Trachez

When the A109 has been in maintenance and before it is flown again in operational missions, the main rotor blade balance has to be measured. This is done by equipment that is temporarily fixed on top of the nose. This is a VXP Sensor and the information obtained by it allows the technicians to adjust the blades if necessary.

Photo: Gert Trachez

Right: A New Zealand AW-109 is landing during an exercise to deliver goods to ground troops. The helicopter can be used to transport Special Forces as well as cargo. Compare this version of the helicopter to the Belgian ones; the forward door is different, it has many different probes, antennas, steps and a dust cover over the engine air intake. Like the Swedish Armed Force's AW-109s, this model has a retractable landing gear. New Zealand operates 6 helicopters of the type, acquired in 2011. They fly with N° 3 Squadron which also operates NH90 helicopters out of RNZAF Base Ohakea, about 120 km north of Wellington.

Photo: Andy Heap

Photo: Robert Pied

Photo: Robert Pied

Left: The base of the wire cutter situated underneath the nose, can be folded up when the helicopter is on the ground. Note the pitot-tube cover.

Photo: Philip Stevens

Photo: Robert Pied

Photo: Robert Pied

Above: A look at the wire cutter on top of the fuselage and the support struts attached to it. On the port side, where the targeting pod used to be, a GPS antenna has been placed.
Right: A view on top of the Agusta's nose. Note the hinges for the two large access doors.

Photo: Gert Trachez

Photo: Robert Pied

Opposite page: The Royal Air Force operates the A109SP within 32 Squadron, based at RAF Northolt. This is the more recent version of the type, equipped with two Pratt & Whitney Canada PW207C turboshaft engines, giving the helicopter a maximum speed of 289 km/h. 32 Squadron is the Royal Squadron, following amalgamation with The Queen's Flight.
Below: Another operator of the A109 is the Italian Guardia di Finanza or the Italian Customs Service, which operates 17 of the type in this smart yellow and green livery. Notice the radar pod underneath the fuselage, typical for this version.

Photo: Philip Stevens

Photo: Gert Trachez

Above: The starboard side of the forward fuselage, which is almost identical to the port side, except for the roof window that is installed over the pilot's seat. Notice the machine guns that are installed in the cargo bay of this helicopter. The Belgian Air Force selected the MAG 7.62 machine gun to give ground forces or descending Special Forces cover when the helicopter is hovering over hostile territory. The crew entrance door can be opened by means of a single handle, while the central part of the window can be slid backwards when necessary.
Right: A close-up of the same helicopter, this time seen inside the maintenance hangar. Notice the moor point and the cover over the engine air intake.
Opposite page: Some details of the A109's fuselage, with the refuelling points, located on either side of the fuselage, the external power hook-up and one of the steps, allowing the crew of technicians to check the engine and main rotor blades.

Photo: Robert Pied

Photo: Robert Pied

Photo: Robert Pied

Photo: Robert Pied

Photo: Gert Trachez

Above: Agusta A109 BA 'H21' sits on the tarmac at Beauvechain Air Base, waiting for another training mission. The large cargo door has been slid back, allowing up to 6 passengers to be transported.

Far Right: The top port fuselage with the engine air intake cover and one of the four engine exhaust pipes.

Photo: Robert Pied

Photo: Robert Pied

Photo: Robert Pied

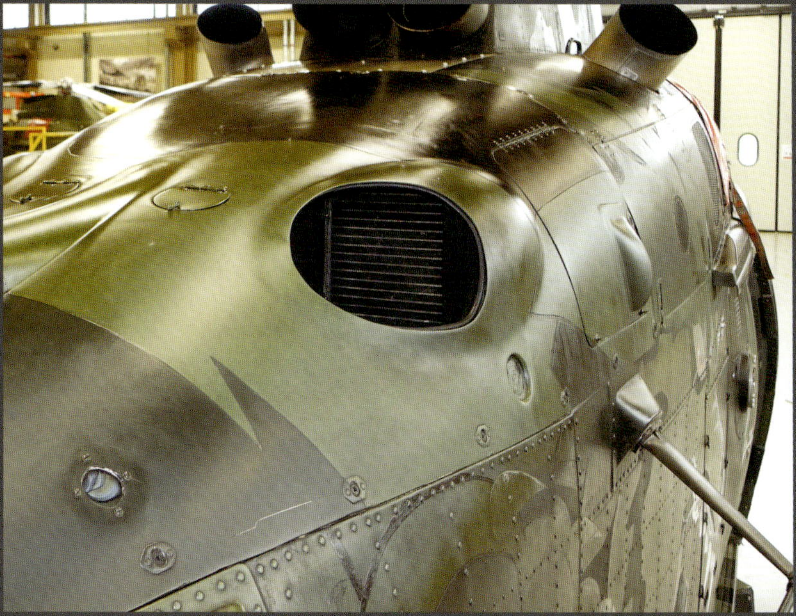

Photo: Robert Pied

Photo: Robert Pied

Above left: A close-up of the starboard engine Oil Cooler Fan, located aft of the four engine exhausts. Although the A109 is equipped with two engines, in the unlikely event of one engine failing, the helicopter can continue to fly safely.

Above: The four Engine Exhaust Pipes in detail. Two are attached to the central part of the top fuselage, while the other two are canted outwards almost immediately behind the engine air intakes.

Left: The starboard fuselage with the closed cargo bay door. Notice that another, smaller window is located aft of the door, giving the passengers flying in the compartment a clear view.

Photo: Peter Anthoni

Above: Early 2000's and A109 H38 is sitting in front of the hangar at Koksijde Air Base. It still carries the markings of the Belgian Army.

Below: The fixture of the Chaff/Flare dispenser, located near the large lateral door on either side of the fuselage.

Photo: Kris Christiaens

Photo: Robert Pied

The A109 can be equipped with pylons on either side of the fuselage that are fixed to the top and bottom of the airframe. These are mostly used for anti-tank missiles, as seen in the photo to the left and below left. In its maximum capacity, two launchers, each containing 2 missiles, can be loaded, giving the helicopter a payload of 8 missiles, which is quite impressive, given the size of the A109. The photo below shows two Belgian A109s with this capacity. Notice the helicopter in the back has a roundel, while the one in front has the national marking on the vertical tail.

Photo: Kris Christiaens

Photo: BAF

Photo: Duke Archives

Photo: Gert Trachez

Photo: Robert Pied

Photo: Robert Pied

Above: This is the UH(L) Medevac version of the A109 BA, as used by the Belgian Air Force. It can easily be recognised by the bulbous fuselage extensions and sliding doors, allowing for one or two stretchers to be placed inside the cargo bay, where a medic and nurse can attend to the wounded soldiers that need to be rushed to the hospital. This version of the helicopter was also used in the aftermath of the gas explosion at Ghislenghien on July 30, 2004, when badly burnt victims needed to be evacuated from the site. 24 people died in the disaster.

Photo: BAF

Photo: Peter Anthoni

Photo: Robert Pied

Left and above: Underneath the fuselage, a large black blade antenna is located. The large wire antenna in the photo to the left is only found on the starboard side of the fuselage. Note the exhaust stains on the aft fuselage.

Photo: Jörgen Nillson

In June 2001 the Swedish Government signed a contract for 20 Agusta A109 LUH-S for the country's Armed Forces. The type is known in Sweden as the Hkp.15A for the Utility variant and Hkp.15B for the Search and Rescue version. The former can be deployed to the Visby class Corvette ships.

In the photo above, an A109LUH seems to be firing in the direction of photographer Jörgen Nillson! This version of the A109 is equipped with a retractable landing gear.

Photo: Jörgen Nillson

Photo: Jörgen Nillson

Photo: Jörgen Nillson

Above: A close-up of the Swedish A109 during a low-level lefthand turn. Notice how different it is from the A109 BA seen on the previous pages. In this version, both the pilot and co-pilot have a window overhead and the pitot-tubes that were located on the side of the nose have been repositionned to the top of the fuselage. With the different engines of the LUH also come different air intakes and engine exhausts. Additional air intakes can be seen in front of the engine bay and on top of the fuselage. Notice the large blade antenna aft of the engine compartment.

Left: A grey Hkp.15B with machine guns in the cargo bay is about to take off. Notice the different style of entrance door.

Photo: Gert Trachez

AgustaWestland A109
Main rotor

Left: Co-pilot Jo Jacobs - then a Captain, now a Sr. Captain - signals to the photographer on the ground, moments before landing. Look at the awesome low-viz Griffin on the side of the aft fuselage.
The A109 helicopter is equipped with a fully-articulated rotor head to which 4 rotor blades are attached by bonded double plates and bonded and bolted grip plates. On top of the rotor head, a round fairing is fixed. The blades themselves are made from aluminium aloy with a honeycomb core. The rotor head is attached to the Main Reduction Gearbox, barely visible underneath it.

Below: This A109 BA has its rotor blades removed - the yellow area in front of the Main Reduction Gearbox houses the Oil Tank on the port side. The black and light grey painted struts support the rotor gearbox. Next to the latter, the Pitch Control Jacks can be seen, allowing the rotorhead to be moved in all directions and thus the helicopter to go in any possible direction.

Photo: Robert Pied

Photo: Yaron Allaert

Main rotor !

The main rotor of the A109 has a diameter of 11 meter. The photo above gives an idea of how large that area really is. The tail rotor, giving balance to the helicopter, is located on the port side of the tail boom.

Right: A close-up of the main rotor, seen from above. Notice the attachment points and large bolts of the aluminium aloy blades to the rotor head. If you look closely, you can see the small oil reservoires attached to each of the Pitch Control actuators, hidden underneath the domed fairing.

Photo: Gert Trachez

Right: A close-up of the main rotor head and the aerodynamic fairing which houses the gear box and pitch control jacks. The oval-shaped grill at the front of the fairing ensures cooling air. On the side of the fairing, a quick release panel is located for easy inspection. The horizontally placed cylinders next to the rotor head towards each rotor blade are shock absorbers.

Below: The main rotor gear box with the cover and blades removed. The top fairing has been removed as well and the holding ring with 5 openings for the bolts can be seen. The bay forward of the gear box is painted yellow chromate and holds the Pitch control Linkage mechanism towards the front of it.

Photo: Gert Trachez

Photo: Robert Pied

Photo: Gert Trachez

Above: Immediately aft of the main rotor, on top of the engine cover, an anti-collision light is located.

Photo: s Christiaens

Tail rotor.

Above: The black and white lines painted on the tailrotor give an idea of the size of the blades on this Medevac version of the A109. Look at all the shades of green and the weathering of the fuselage of this helicopter.

Photo: Robert Pied

The tail rotor of the A109 produces horizontal thrust in the same direction of the main rotor's rotation in order to counter the reactional torque exerted on the fuselage by the latter. Without the tail rotor, the helicopter would be simply spinning around its axis in the opposite direction of the main rotor's rotation. The pilot controls the pitch of the tail rotor by means of the anti-torque pedals. He uses these to turn the helicopter when it is hovering.

Right: The two-bladed tail rotor of H46, the A109 BA of the Belgian Air Force Demo Team, sporting the 30th anniversary logo. Like the main rotor blades, the tail rotor blades are made out of aluminium aloy with a honeycomb core.

Photo: Gert Trachez

Photo: Gert Trachez

Photo: Gert Trachez

Photo: Gert Trachez

Above: The horizontal part in between the tail rotor blades and the vertical tail is the control mechanism. It is connected to the tail rotor gear box. The pitch of the blades allows to change the amount of thrust they produce.

Photo: Gert Trachez

Time to get a closer look at the cockpit of the A109, where the pilot sits on the right and the co-pilot in the left seat. These photos were taken from a Belgian Air Force A109 BAi. The “i” stands for “instrument”, refering to the glass instruments that were introduced during an update of the helicopter. Because of this modification, the A109 was able to also fly IFR. On top of the central instrument panel, on the right, the G-meter can be seen, with to the left of it the panel that allows to drop chaff or flares. The main instruments are repeated for both crew members, such as the Artificial Horizon, Altimeter and Airspeed Indicator. Notice the multifunction displays with keyboard on the panel and in between the two seats.

Photo: Robert Pied

Above: The pedals that control the pitch of the tail rotor, allowing the helicopter to go left or right.

Photo: Peter Anthoni

Photo: Robert Pied

Photo: Robert Pied

Top: Both pilot and co-pilot can control a flight stick in front of them and the horizontally placed Cyclic Pitch Control to the left of them. The entire cockpit section of the A109 is painted black.

Right: A look at the cockpit roof, seen standing at the port side of the helicopter. The A109 BA, such as used by the Belgian Air Force, only has a cockpit roof window on the starboard side, which is where the pilot sits. Central on the ceiling, the overhead instrument panel is located with at the front of it the rotation brake. More to the aft, dials, light switches and the windscreen wiper controls are located. Even more aft, a large number of circuit breakers can be found.
On either side of the overhead panel, a cockpit light is placed.

Photo: Robert Pied

Photo: Robert Pied

Photo: Gert Trachez

Above: A close-up of the co-pilot's Cyclic Pitch Control lever, with the flight stick next to it. The latter is shown in detail in the cut-out photo to the right. Notice that the seats and other cockpit equipment have been removed from the helicopter which was sitting in the large maintenance hangar at Beauvechain Air Base.

Photo: Gert Trachez

The view from the cockpit of the A109 is excellent; next to the windscreen and door windows, each pilot has a floor window, allowing them to see how close to the ground they are flying or hovering, which comes in handy, especially during landing. Only the pilot of the A109 BA has a roof window, however most other versions of the A(W)109, have an overhead window for both pilots.

At the top of the instrument panel, a large number of warning lights are located. See that the helicopter in this photo has a speed of just over 100 knots and has 240 kg of fuel remaining? Notice that the chaff/flare panel is missing in the cockpit of this helicopter. Engine oil temperature, oil pressure, hydraulic pressure and fuel pressure seem to be exactly the way they should be.

Photo: Robert Pied

Photo: Gert Trachez

Top Left: The helicopter's engines run at constant speed - the engine controls are located at the front of the overhead panel. The two round black levers are basically the throttles of the helicopter, which have 3 positions: 'Off', 'Idle' or 'Flight', for which the handles have to be pushed fully forward. Halfway the lever, the starter button is located.

Photo: Peter Anthoni

Above: "Comfy" seats for the flight crew with four-point seatbelts neatly stowed. On longer flights, they proved to be uhm ... less comfy...

Right: A close-up of the overhead light for the pilot in the left seat.

Photo: Robert Pied

Photo: Gert Trachez

Photo: Gert Trachez

Above: The port access door to the cockpit in close-up, with a compartment for documents or maps, the door handle and sliding side window. Notice the actuator that fixes the door to the floor of the helicopter.

Right: Before the crew flies away in their A109, a checklist has to be followed; Parking Brake? On. Landing Lights? Off. Anti-collision Lights? On. Position Lights? On. Anti-icing? Off. And so on. Even though for experienced pilots, it seems to be routine, this is an important part of the start-up, during which the crew gets into a professional mode. Necessary, because flying a helicopter is serious business and a good preparation is essential.

Photo: Robert Pied

Left: The overhead panel, seen from the pilot's seat. In front of the circuit breakers, the lighting panel and battery switches are located. The lighting panel controls the light of the instruments, but also the anti-collision and position lights. The red switches you see on the right side of the panel are the switches for the battery, generators 1 and 2, generator bus 1 and 2 and two inverters, which provide power for the avionics running on AC instead of DC power. Later model A109s have 3 inverters, but not all of them to be switched on at the same time. By pushing the starter buttons, the first stage of the turbine starts to spin, allowing air to move through the engines. When the engines run at 15 percent, the throttle is moved forward to 'Idle' and fuel is injected into the combustion chamber. At this point the temperature will rise, which should be monitored, because the turbine is still too slow to cool the engines.

Photo: Robert Pied

Photo: Robert Pied

Right: Another overal view of the cockpit, with the seats removed. During start-up, the engines are put up to 'Flight' one by one and before take off, the hydraulics and the flight controls are checked. Taxiing towards the take off position, the ground steering is done with the pedals. The A109 is a comfortable helicopter to fly and this is one of the reasons why so many of them have been bought by both military and civilian operators. With a cruising speed of around 120-140 knots depending on the specific aircraft configuration, the helicopeter is ideal to quickly cover short distances, even though it has a maximum range of slightly over 900 km.

Photo: Robert Pied

Photo: Wim Houquet

Left: This photo shows the cockpit of an AW-109 of the Swedish Armed Forces - look how different it is from the original cockpit of the A109 shown above. The instrument panel is dominated by the large multi-functional displays. Notice also the different control stick used in this version of the helicopter. The lower side-windows give the crew a much better look at what is happening below them, which comes in very handy during hovering. Near the bottom of the page, you can see the differently shaped pedals. To the edges of the instrument panel, a compass is located on either side.

Photo: Robert Pied

Let's have a quick look inside the cargo or passenger compartment, immediately aft of the cockpit. The photos on this page show it with the gun fixtures installed on either side of the bay. In this configuration, a pair of MAG 7.62 machine guns are carried by the Belgian Air Force machines. It isn't the biggest gun around, but very reliable and it leaves a nasty sting to whomever is on the receiving end. Notice the bags attached to the fixtures, which will catch the empty gun shells. Contrary to the cockpit, the aft compartment is light grey all over, with sound isolation material on the ceiling. When no guns are necessary, additional aft facing seats can be installed.

Photo: Robert Pied

Photo: Robert Pied

Photo: Robert Pied

Left: The inside of the sliding cargo door and its handle in detail. Notice the air conditioning vents above it and the step on the lower fuselage, which is painted black.

Above: In order to communicate with the pilots, a radio box and control system is located near the ceiling of the compartment, on the left side.

Photo: Robert Pied

Photo: Robert Pied

Above and left: The cargo compartment with just the back seats installed, allowing for 3 fully equipped Ground Forces to be seated. As mentionned before, guns or additional seats can be installed.

Photo: Gert Trachez

Above: This A109 is about to land and has the landing lights illuminated. The Belgian A109s have a fixed landing gear.

Right: The modern versions of the AW109 have a retractable landing gear, however much of the wheels themselves are left out of the fuselage to safe space. These photos show the nosegear of an AW109 of the Swedish Armed Forces.

Photo: Wim Houquet

Photo: Wim Houquet

Early versions of the A109 have a fixed landing gear, which can be seen here in detail. When towing the helicopter, this is where the equipment is hooked up, but first the nose wheel has to be unlocked. The nose wheel is equipped with a hydraulic shock absorber. Contrary to the tires of an aircraft, a helicopter's tires don't have to be changed all that often. Softer landings, you see.

Photo: Robert Pied

Photo: Robert Pied

Photo: Gert Trachez

Photo: Peter Anthoni

Photo: Robert Pied

Above: H27 of the Belgian Air Force is hovering, ready to touch down. Notice that this helicopter is still carrying the faded indication 'Force Terrestre' on the aft fuselage. On the other side of the fuselage, the same is written in Dutch, one of the other official languages of the country. Of interest are the different shades of green on this helicopter and the stained aft fuselage. Look at the large curved tailskid.

Right: A look from underneath the fuselage towards where the main landing gear is fixed. Notice the drains next to it.

Photo: Gert Trachez

Photo: Gert Trachez

Above: The starboard main landing gear seen from the side. Notice the wiring to the aft of it. When on the ground, the shock absorber of the main gear is completely compressed. When the landing gear has to be removed during maintenance, the Goodyear tires first have to be deflated.

Right: Notice the double connection to the fuselage of the main wheel vertical strut in this photo. It also shows the large black blade antenna located underneath the fuselage.
The A109 is known as a small, but fast helicopter and some versions of it even hold world records. In 2008, a standard AW109S Grand set a new record by flying around the world in 11 days, 7 hours and 2 minutes.

Photo: Robert Pied

Photo: Robert Pied

Above: The main landing gear of an A109 seen from above. Notice the cables attached to the wheel to the back of it.

Left: The starboard main landing gear of an A109 sitting in the maintenance hangar.

Photo: Robert Pied

Above: The port main landing gear, seen from the back. In this photo, the cables running towards it can be seen to good effect.

Left: The brand new port main landing gear tire needs 6 bar of air pressure. It is placed in a fixed position, unlike with other helicopters, such as the Lynx.

Photo: Robert Pied

AgustaWestland A109
Main Landing Gear

Photo: Wim Houquet

Left: This RAF AW-109, about to land, has a retractable landing gear. Notice how the landing lights, which in the older version of the helicopter are placed in the nose, are repositionned in the horizontal base of the main landing gear. Look at the cut-out for the nose wheel in the two gear doors.

Below: Unlike the Belgian A109s, the Swedish Armed Forces helicopters are equipped with a retractabel landing gear. This spectacular photo by Jörgen Nillson shows the entire belly of the helicopter with the gear retracted, with the main gear folded inwards and the nosewheel forward. Notice how the latter has about half of the wheel passing from the fuselage, with the gear doors around it. Look at all the details on the underside of the fuselage and the gun showing through the starboard cabin door. Also notice the glass floor of the cockpit, giving the pilots the possibility to see directly below them. Notice the national markings on the horizontal tails.

Photo: Jörgen Nillson

Photo: Gert Trachez

Vertical tail

Above: With the landing lights on, H28 is about to land during a training mission. This particular helicopter entered service within the Belgian Air Force in June 1993 and remains in active duty till this day. Notice how heavily the tail boom and vertical tail are stained from the engine exhausts. The green position light on the horizontal tail is on. During landings, the helicopter's nose is pulled up and to avoid the tail rotor from hitting the ground, a large and sturdy tailskid is installed underneath the vertical tail. To the right is a close-up of the attachment point of the tailskid. In later models of the A(W)109, the skid is placed in a aerodynamic cover.

Photo: Robert Pied

Right: This photo shows the sence of the tailskid on the A(W)109 during landings. The vertical tail was redesigned, with the tip being larger and horizontal. On the port side of the aft fuselage, a lateral streak is placed, while the engine exhausts are larger and reduced from four to two. In the middle of them, a large blade antenna is positioned. The top anti-collision light is also repositionned.

Photo: Jörgen Nillson

Below: Seen at Oostende Airport in Belgium, this brand new AW109 is on its way to be delivered to the Swedish Armed Forces. Notice the modified shape of the vertical tail and the differently shaped tailskid. Notice the DC-8 in the background. Now there's something you don't see every day!

Photo: Wim Houquet

Photo: Gert Trachez

Photo: Robert Pied

A closer look at the tailskid preventing the tail rotor blades from hitting the ground during landing. Notice the base of the high voltage antenna on the aft fuselage in the photo above.

Photo: Robert Pied

hoto: Gert Trachez

Photo: Gert Trachez

Photo: Robert Pied

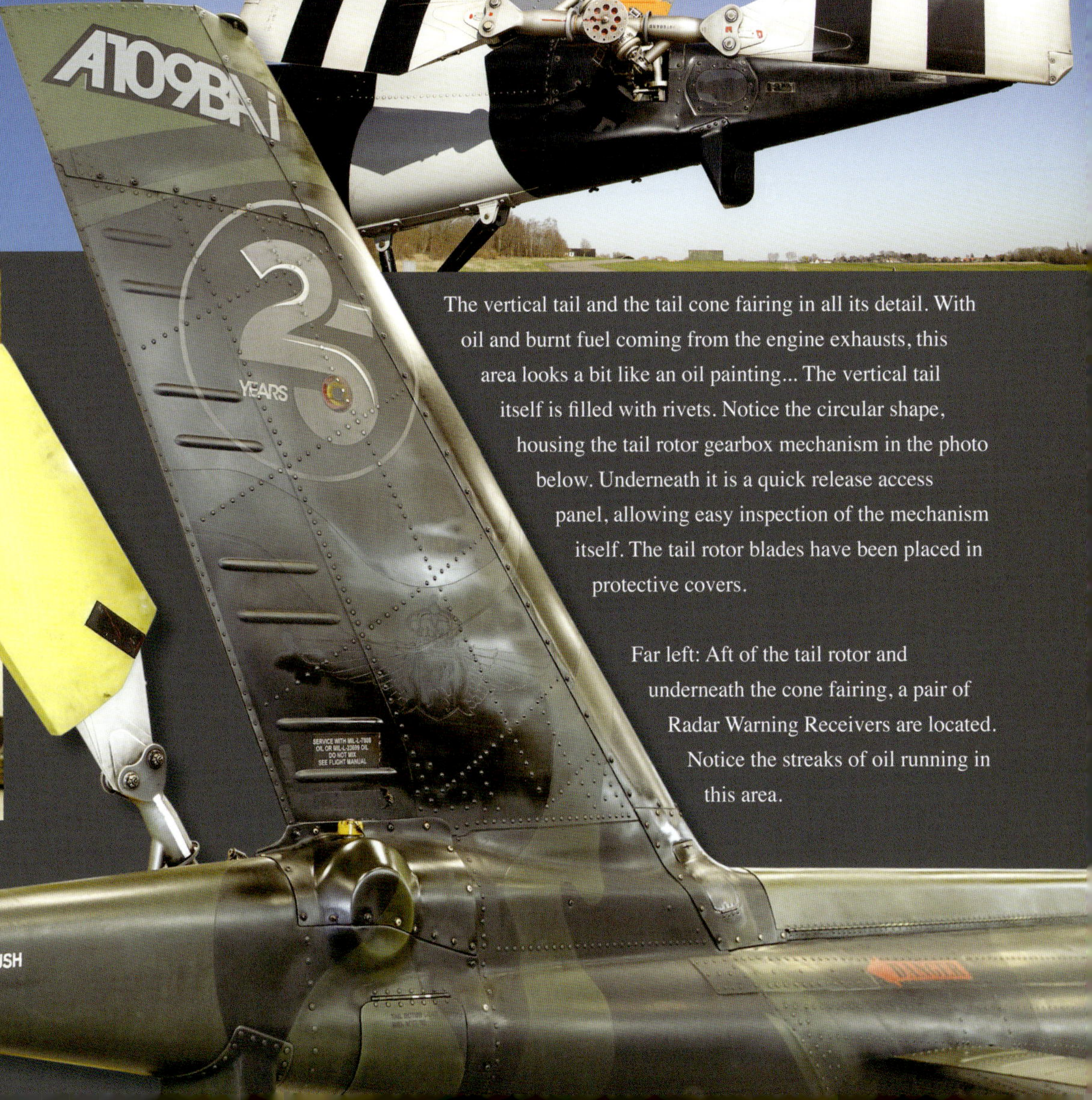

The vertical tail and the tail cone fairing in all its detail. With oil and burnt fuel coming from the engine exhausts, this area looks a bit like an oil painting... The vertical tail itself is filled with rivets. Notice the circular shape, housing the tail rotor gearbox mechanism in the photo below. Underneath it is a quick release access panel, allowing easy inspection of the mechanism itself. The tail rotor blades have been placed in protective covers.

Far left: Aft of the tail rotor and underneath the cone fairing, a pair of Radar Warning Receivers are located. Notice the streaks of oil running in this area.

Photo: Robert Pied

Photo: Arne Mathijs

Above: From this angle, the horizontal tail can be seen to good effect. On the extremities of these, a position light is placed; green for the starboard side, red on the port side. The switches to turn them on are located on the overhead panel in the cockpit. The pilot has also illuminated the landing lights in the nose of the helicopter.

Right: On top of the tail boom, the tail rotor transmission shaft is located, which is housed in a semi-circular cover. This cover folds to starboard, allowing inspection by technicians.

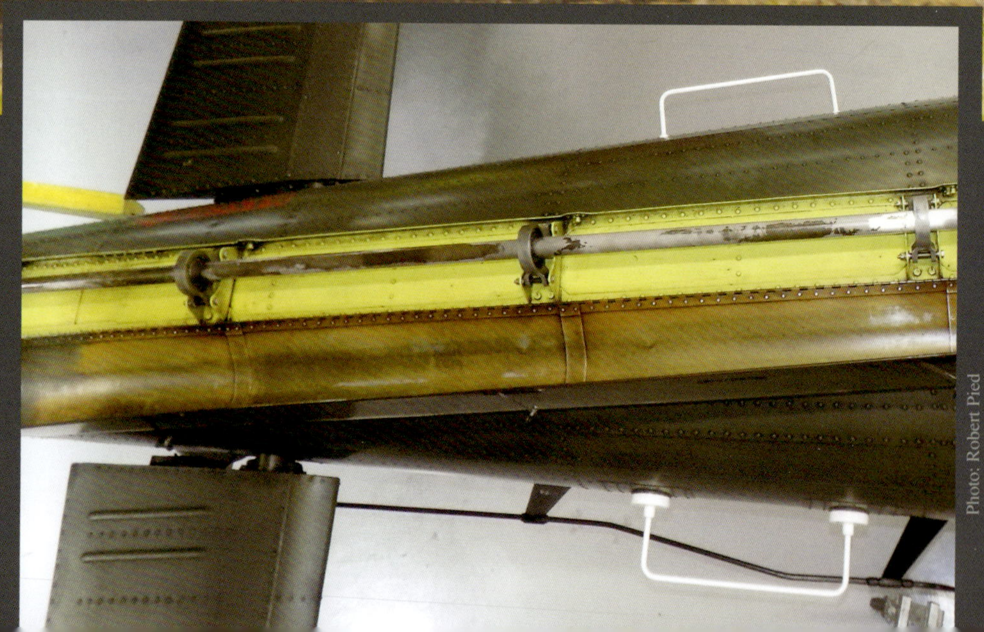

Photo: Robert Pied

Photo: Robert Pied

Left: The attachment hinge to the horizontal tails of the Agusta A109, with the shaft slightly visible. When in maintenance, these elevators are also covered to avoid damage.

Below left: Another look at this area, also showing the tail rotor transmission shaft. Interior parts of the helicopter are painted in chrome yellow primer, allowing to easily see leaks or damage.

Below: A close-up of the green starboard position light on the horizontal tails extremity.

Photo: Robert Pied

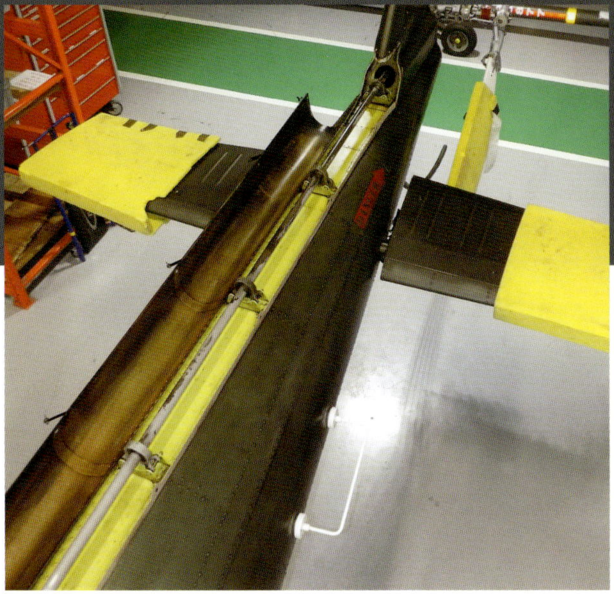

Photo: Gert Trachez

Photo: Gert Trachez

Maintenance

It is a long standing tradition in our books to include an extensive chapter on the maintenance of our subjects. Not only is it appreciated by the modellers among you, but it is also a tribute to the technicians, engineers and software specialists that ensure the reliability of the aircraft or helicopters they work on. Their work should never be taken for granted, especially by the pilots. It isn't an exageration to say that without the hard work being done in the maintenance hangars, there would be no flying.

So let's have a closer look at the A109 in maintenance. For this, we visited Beauvechain on several occasions, allowing us to show you the helicopter in various states of maintenance. Like H38 in the photo above, which has its engine covers and main rotor blades removed. The crew entrance doors have also been removed for some reason. Even though fold-down step are located on the fuselage, it is easier to do some serious work on the helicopter by placing custom made platforms next to it.

Right: The engine bay with the engines removed, seen from the starboard side of the helicopter. Notice the 4 engine exhausts.

Below: Here's a vital piece of equipment that can be found in the maintenance hangar at Beauvechain Air Base in Belgium: aluminum boxes placed around the landing gear. When I asked about it, I wasn't expecting this answer: these are to prevent mice from crawling up on the gear and knibbling on the cables... There are two cats kept in the hangar as well, but they are not all that interested in hunting the mice, it seems.

Photo: Gert Trachez

Photo: Robert Pied

Photo: Robert Pied

Left: The main rotor head seen from below, with the 5 meter long rotor blades removed. Notice that next to each blade attachment, horizontally placed cylinders can be seen. These are rotor blade shock absorbers. Clearly visible in this photo are two of the three Pitch Control Jacks.

The nose of the helicopter has two large quick-release doors allowing easy access to the equipment stowed there. The doors remain open by means of a thin strut attached to to cockpit bulckhead. The compartment is filled with avionics systems; in civilian operated A(W)109s, the helicopter's batteries can be found to the right in this area. On the doors, a white circle with a red cross can be seen and in the photo below right, you can see why: this is where a green first aid medical equipment kit is stowed. Notice all the wiring running from the avionics through the bulckhead towards the instrument panel.

Photo: Peter Anthoni

Photo: Peter Anthoni

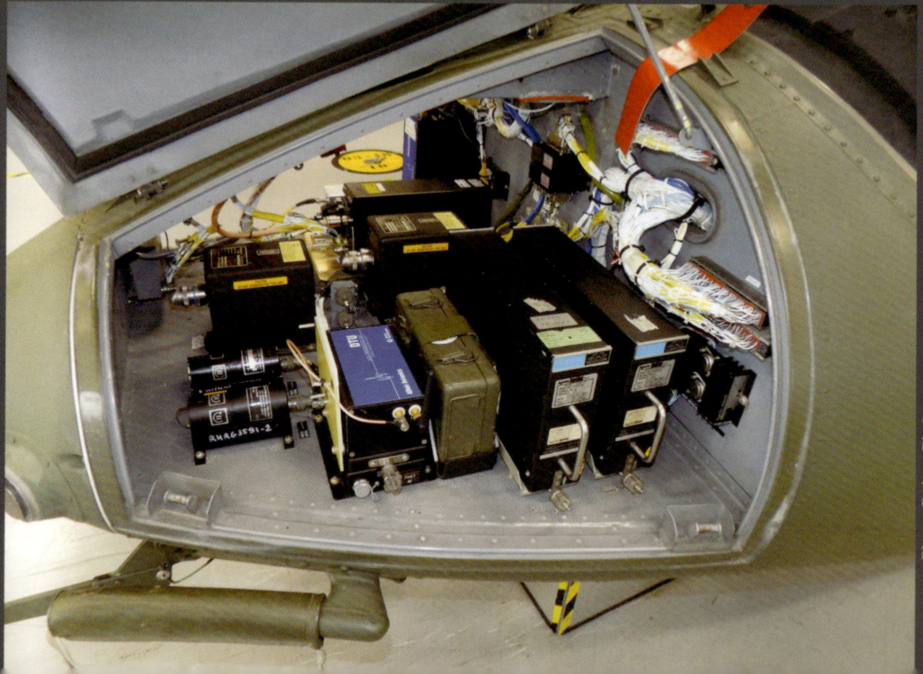

Photo: Robert Pied

Photo: Robert Pied

Photo: Robert Pied

Photo: Robert Pied

Photo: Robert Pied

Photo: Robert Pied

Standing on a platform to the left side of the helicopter, this is what you can see from the main rotor gear box and the area in front of it. The chromate yellow interior allows a quick overal check of leaks or damage. On the left side, a large oil tank can be seen. Aft of this and also seen in the photo below, is the opening for the engine's air intake. Immediately below that, the Refuelling point can be seen. The helicopter has two refuelling points and L-shaped fuel tanks, allowing for a maximum of 550 liters of fuel. Note the hand hold below the engine compartment.

Photo: Robert Pied

Photo: Robert Pied

Right: The large Oil Cooler fans with the drive shaft for the tail rotor in between them.

Below: The area in front of the main rotor gear box, this time seen from the starboard side. Notice the round air intake tubing in this area. To the front of the compartment, the Pitch Control Linkage Mechanism can be seen. The gearbox itself is fixed to the fuselage by means of 4 struts; two grey ones on the port side, two black ones on the starboard side.

Photo: Robert Pied

oto: Robert Pied

Photo: Robert Pied

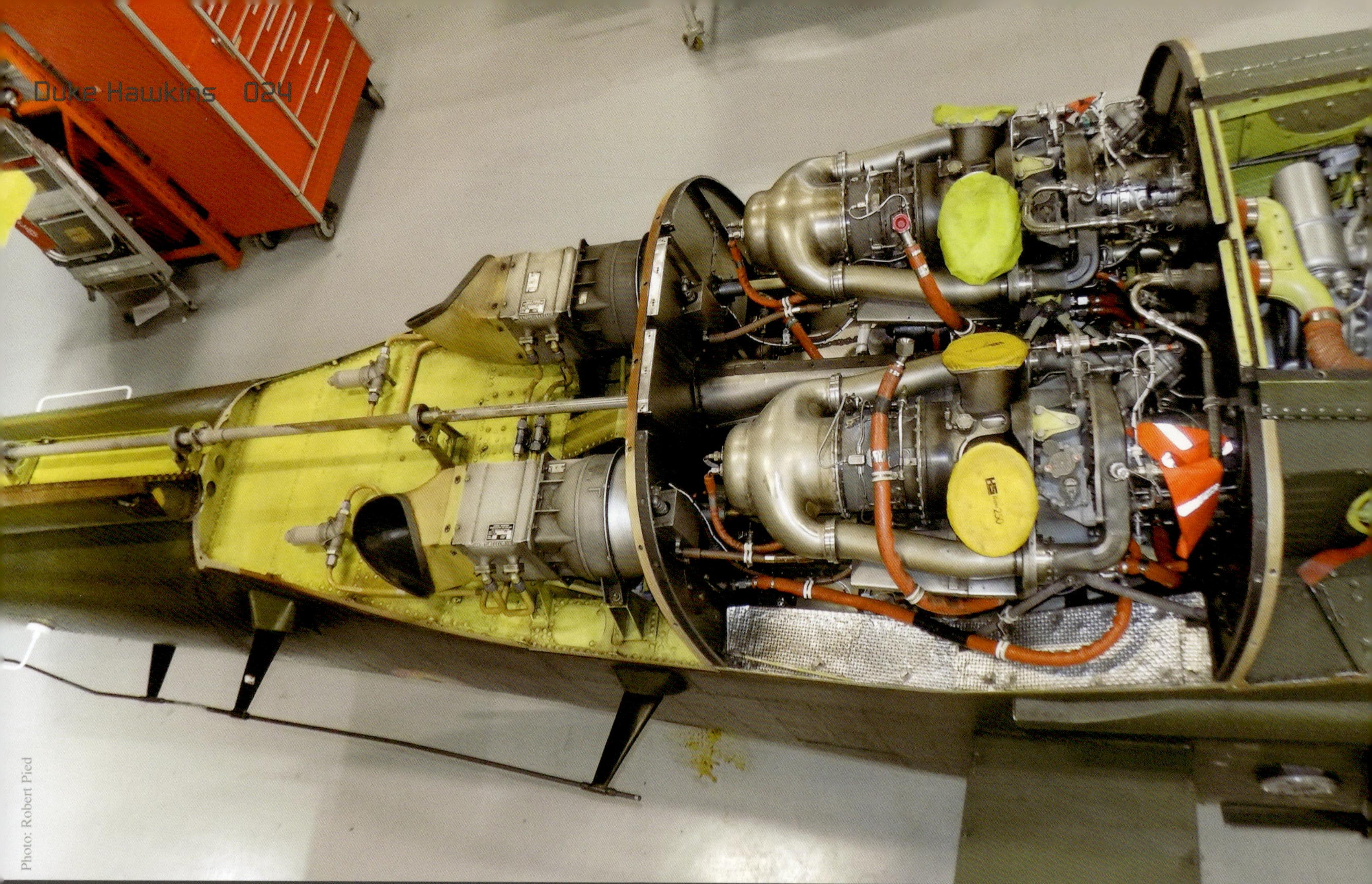

Photo: Robert Pied

Above: This photo shows the two engines powering the A109 BA - you can clearly see where the four engine exhaust pipes will be fixed once it is time to put the helicopter back together after maintenance. On the starboard side of the aft fuselage, the black high voltage antenna is located.

Right: Another look at the same area, this time seen from above and standing on the port side. You can just see the Engine Transmission shaft running in between the two engines. The engines are placed in a stainless steel compartment, but no firewall is placed in between them.

Photo: Robert Pied

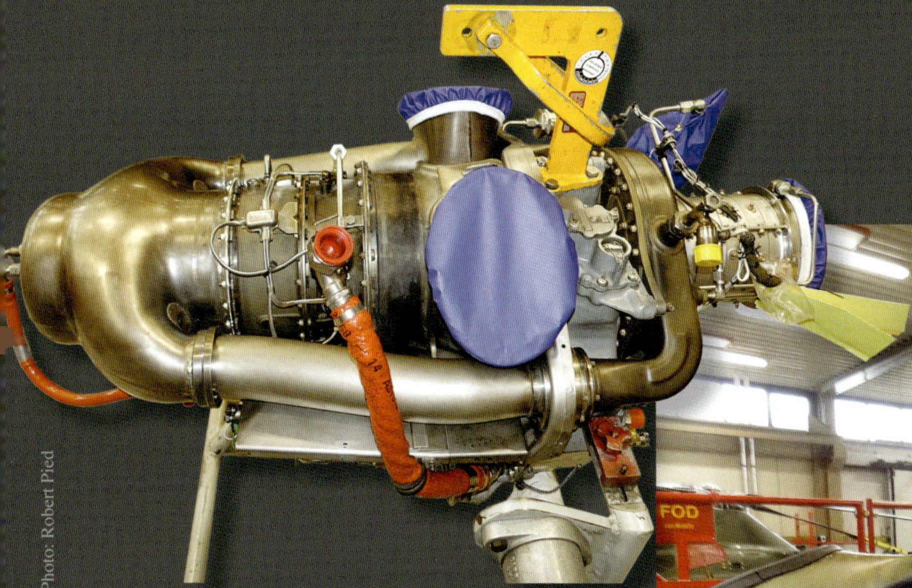

Photo: Robert Pied

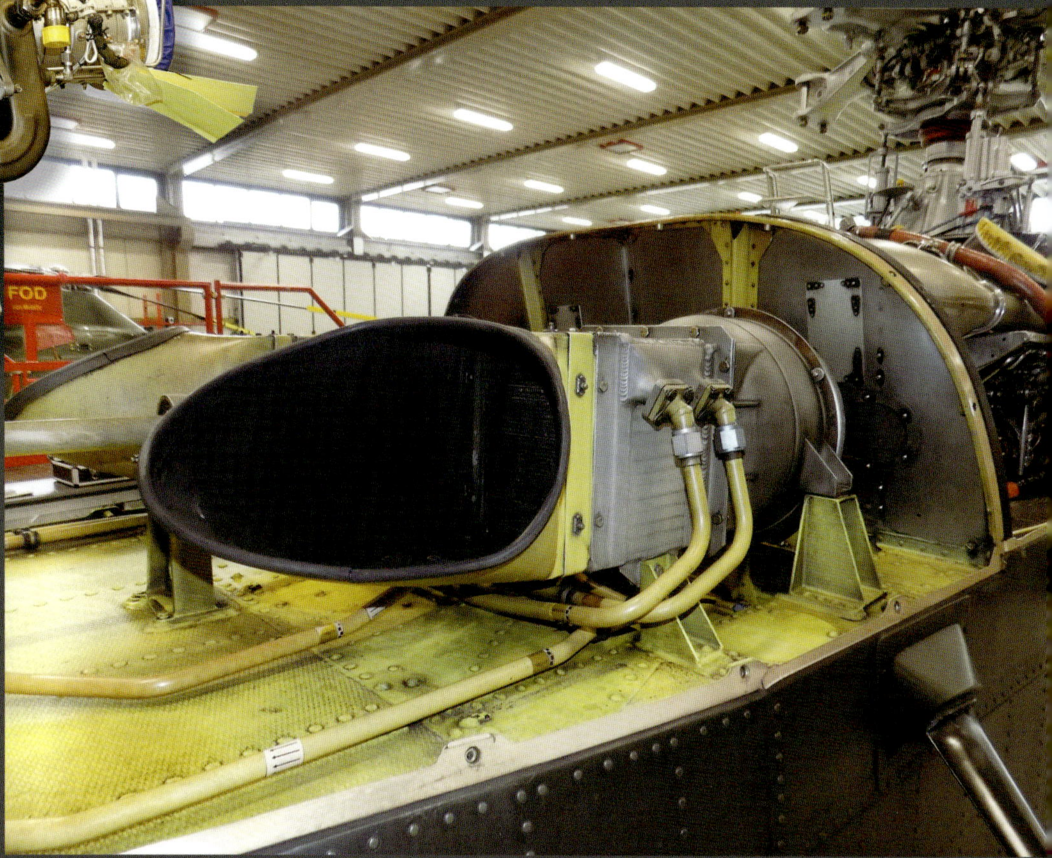

Above: The Allison Model 250 engine was developped in the 1960s and has proven to be a reliable and popular engine for small helicopters and aircraft. It is just under 1 meter long and has a dry weight of 63 kg. It produces some 317 hp - each - with an overall pressure ratio of 6.2:1. It comprises of 6-stage axial and 1-stage centrifugal compressors and a single can combustion chambre. The engine runs on standard JP-4 kerosene.

oto: Robert Pied

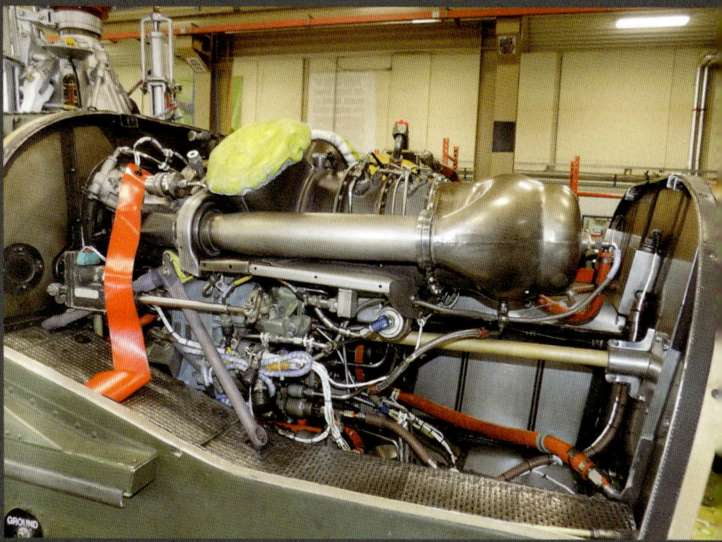

Photo: Robert Pied

Photo: Robert Pied

Photo: Robert Pied

These photos show the tail rotor assembly with the tailcone fairing removed. Above and right is the tail rotor gearbox and control mechanisme, while the two photos below show the drive shaft for the tail rotor and where it fits into the gearbox.

Photo: Robert Pied

Photo: Robert Pied

Photo: Robert Pied

Photo: Robert Pied

On the aft fuselage, on both sides, a stowage compartment is located, which houses more avionics equipment on the starboard side and maintenance equipment in the port one. The interior of this area is uncharacteristically painted light grey. The photo below right gives a view inside the tail boom, with all the electrical wiring running through it.

Photo: Robert Pied

Photo: Robert Pied

Photo: Gert Trachez

Above: An A109 BA which used to be the Demo Team's helicopter before '46' was painted, is being pushed out of the maintenance hangar. Job well done!

Right: The large access door to the avionics compartment on the port side also houses the external power hook up.

Far right: The same area, but this time with the large door opened and the battery removed.

Photo: Robert Pied

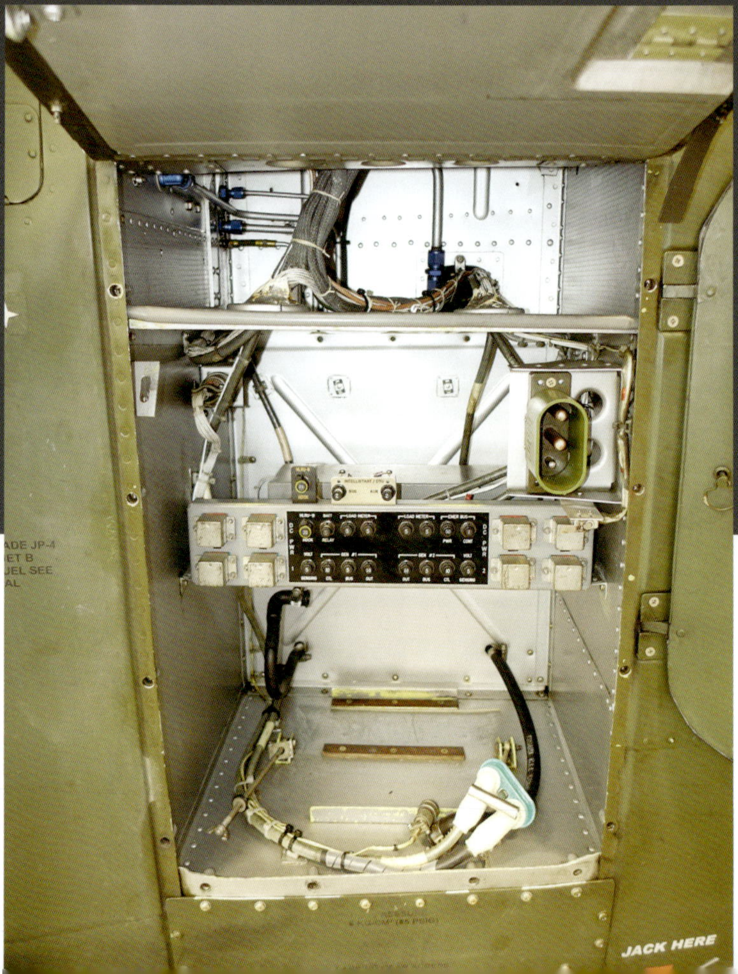

Photo: Robert Pied

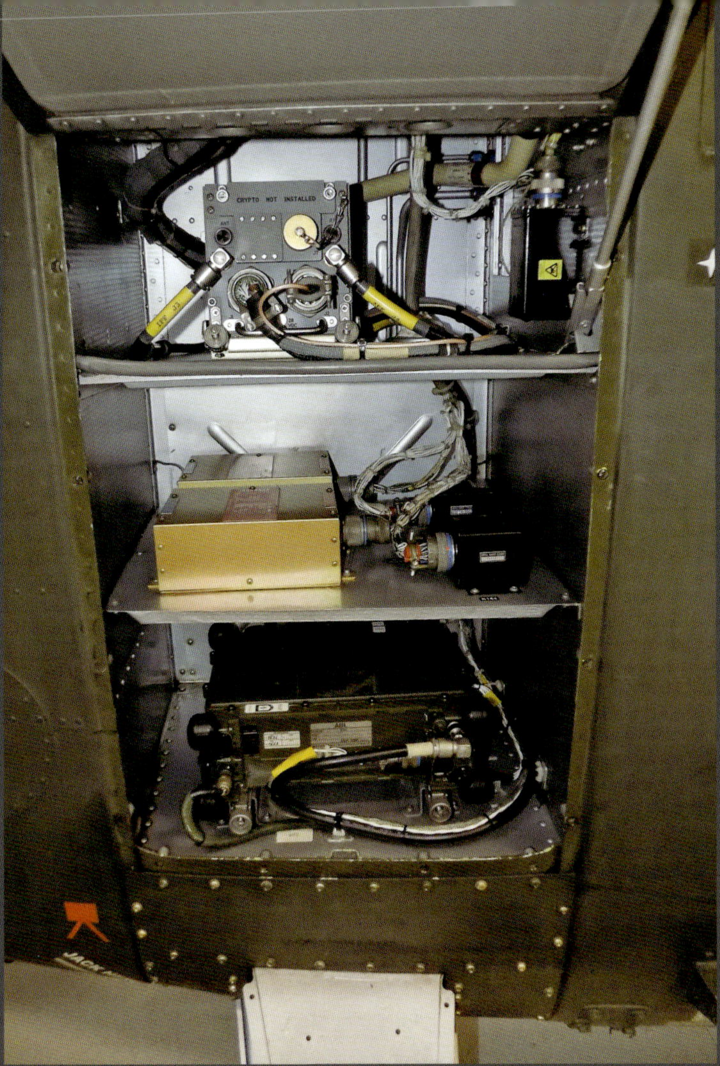

Photo: Robert Pied

Photo: Robert Pied

Photo: Robert Pied

Above & above left: The fuselage equipment bay on the starboard side of the fuselage. The lower part of it houses a battery that is used for starting the engines. A strut attached to the front of it keeps the bay open. Immediately in front of it is the starboard refuelling point with below it the L-shaped fuel tank for the JP-4 kerosene.

Left: The aft part of the main rotor head fairing is waiting to be reattached to the top of the fuselage. On top of it is the anti-collision light and to the back the opening for two of the four engine exhaust pipes.

Action !

Photo: Kris Christiaens

Time for some action! And because the little helicopter can be given many different tasks, the action shows the versatility of the Agusta A109. The photo above pictures a Medevac version of the A109 BA during an international exercise with Belgian Special Forces. A “wounded” soldier, holding his weapon firmly to his body, is on a stretcher and about to be loaded in the helicopter while a medic is ready to take care of him. During the operation, one of the Special Forces is keeping a close eye on our photographer Kris Christiaens... Better keep your distance, Kris !

Right: The Belgian Air Force Agustas have been operating discretely for 3 decades, mostly in the shadow of other types, like the F-16, C-130 or Sea King, but that doesn't mean that they weren't deployed to many different countries. Here, H31 is hovering somewhere over the mountainous terrain of the French pyrenees. The helicopters have seen action in every imaginable terrain and conflict, bringing passangers, equipment and Special Forces safely from one point to another.

Photo: BAF

Below: A quick check of the engine before taking off on another mission. Winter or summer, the reliable helicopter is always ready for action. Note how close the air intake is to the engine.

Photo: Jozef Vanden Broeck

Photo: Andy Heap

Above: The Royal New Zealand Air Force is another operator of the type, which is designated A109LUH - Light Utility Helicopter. Like its Swedish counterpart, this type is equipped with a retractable landing gear and a winch on the starboard side of the cargo bay. Today, 5 of them are flown in 3 Squadron and are mainly used to train future helicopter pilots before they transition to the NH90 or SH-2 Super Seasprite.

Right: A pair of A109s is about to land somewhere in the fields, ready to pick up special forces and one of their wounded comerades. The A109s have been working discretely for 30 years in the Belgian Air Force.

Below: A Swedish Armed Forces AW109 makes a low level left hand turn with its landing gear retracted. Look at the different style of engine exhausts, the streak on the aft fuselage and the different top of the fin.

Photo: Kris Christiaens

Photo: Jörgen Nillson

Photo: Jörgen Nillson

Photo: Jozef Vanden Broeck

Above: The Swedish Armed Forces have two types of the AW109 in service. This is a Hkp.15B that can be operated from ships. To the side of the fuselage, flotation devices are installed. Note the different type of air intakes and engine exhausts, as well as the retractable landing gear.

Left: A pair of Belgian A109 BA's are sitting in the early morning on the tarmac, waiting for the crews to arrive.

Right: Pointing its nose down and shooting flares. The Belgian A109s are equipped with Radar Warning Receivers on the nose and at the rear, immediately below the vertical tail on the tail fairing. These RWRs can detect radar guided missiles.
In order to spot heat seeking missiles, the crew has to count on the human eyeball 2.0.
When such a weapon is heading towards the helicopter, the heat produced by the flares will distract the missile's seeker.
Instead of going after the heat of the helicopter's engines, the missile will go for the flares, while the pilots take evasive action.

Right: Another operator of the A109 is the South African Air Force. This helicopter is an A109 LUH and is part of 17 Squadron, based at Swartkop, Pretoria. The unit is responsable for transport, Search and Rescue and Utility missions. Painted in a very cool camouflage scheme, the helicopter has some interesting features, such as the Radar Warning Receivers on the nose and the steps underneath of the cargo bay. Notice the long streak on the tail boom and the cover to the base of the tail skid. 17 Squadron was formed in 1939 and has flown some legendary aircraft, such as the Junkers Ju-52, Bristol Blenheim V, Vickers Wellington and T-6 Harvard. After the T-6, the unit transferred to helicopters, like the S-55, S-51, Alouette II and III.

Photo: Gert Trachez

Right: During international exercises, the Belgian A109s are often used as an observation platform, as seen in this photo. On the ground, a German radar vehicle can be seen, partially hiden by the vegitation.

Opposite page: One of the most spectacular moments during the display of the Belgain Air Force A109 Demo Team, is when a large number of flares are dropped, especially during sunset air shows. This spectacular photo by Gert Trachez was taken at the Sanicole air show in Belgium. The two flare dispensers are located underneath the fuselage, below the cargo doors.

Photo: Kris Christiaens

Photo: Kris Christiaens

Left: A pair of Belgian Air Force Agustas is returning to their home base of Beauvechain. H35 is in the lead, while its wingman has the Griffon of the squadron painted on the aft fuselage. Notice how the aft fuselage is stained by the engine exhausts. The Belgian Air Force is looking to replace the ageing A109s and one of the possibilities would be the Airbus H145, a reliable helicopter of which over 1,500 have been produced to date.

Right: Between 2000 and 2008 the US Coast Guard operated 8 A109E helicopters, which received the designation MH-68A Stingray. This photo shows one of those, attached to the Helicopter Interdiction Tactical Squadron - HITRON - patrolling the harbour of Los Angeles. Their task is to intercept drug couriers and support Home Land Security. The MH-68A was equipped with a winch, emergency floats on the side of the fuselage, a Forward Looking InfraRed - FLIR - and a strong search light.

Photo: US Coadt Guard

Photo: BAF

Photo: Bart Rosselle

Above: 2017 and elements of 1 Wing of the Belgian Air Force deployed to Gabon in central Africa for Tropical Storm, a joint exercise with the Belgian Army. Special Forces operated from the newly acquired NH90 TTH helicopters and a C-130 Hercules transport aircraft. An A109 in medevac configuration was part of the package in case some of the Special Forces men got injured. This photo shows two of the NH90 Caiman flying in formation with A109 H22 over the delta of the Ogooué river in the most western part of the country. Look at the aft fuselage, stained from the four engine exhausts and the wider part of the forward fuselage, typical for this version of the A109.

Photo: Laurent Heyligen

Duke Hawkins

While some aircraft or helicopters have hundreds of books written about hem, others can be around for decades and still no-one publishes anything about them. The AgustaWestand is of the latter category. With this 24th book in our series, I hope to change that. The A(W) 109 is an interesting and photogenic little helicopter that fifty years after its first flight is still widely used and in production. This book wouldn't have been possible without the generous help provided by Jo Jacobs and Stijn Soenens, the pilots of the Belgian Air Force "Razzle Blades" Display Team. They are true ambassadors for the Air Force: accessible, humble and always ready to talk to people who are interested in starting a career within the Belgian Air Force. While for the walkaround part of this book, editor Robert Pied made the majority of the photos, the first part of the book, which focusses on the Display Team, was very much a group effort. For this part, the Team requested their many followers and aircraft enthusiasts to send photos and they did in large numbers. Some of the photos were used in this book, but I want to thank everyone who reacted to the call of J.J. and Stijn.

It is exactly 5 years since our first book on the Sepecat Jaguar was released. What an adventure it has been! I hope we can continue on this journey and that you will remain interested in the series!

Duke